On the Horizon
prose poems

Joanne Penney

Cover image by Simon Berger

Copyright © 2021 Joanne Penney

All rights reserved.

ISBN: 978-0-6450417-7-4 (paperback)
ISBN: 978-0-6450417-6-7 (ebook)

penneywrites@gmail.com

For Bec,

1973 - 2021

For the friendship, and for insisting

I never hide your name in my words.

Bec - a portrait

Flowing garments of teal, black and purple cling and wrap about skin bursting to fly away, inked in butterflies and skulls, gangster hippiness climbs up your arms and across your back, under deep dyed hair of blood, perpetually wool blind in front of baby blues. Rock star sunglasses worn as a crown reveal hoops aplenty, silver ears, jewels on gnarled fingers, nails bitten to the quick. Those butterflies of yours took flight, reproduced, yet those names will never be ink on your skin, though inked upon your heart. You entered your own chrysalis, cathartic rest reward, for you, the mother, daughter, grandmother, had one metaphoric metamorphosis left to make and with wings of teal, black and purple soar (to new adventures) far above my tears.

Rose

Nimble fingers work the fabric, match the up and down of chevron lines. She tacks the piece in place to double check. If only this could be a perfect garment, if only. Needle through fabric, and into finger. Delicate shiny bubble of life, crimson, sits atop perfectly like a jewel. Red does not belong on black and white, mostly white. Frantic, she finds a scrap, just half the pattern, no longer a zig-zag but just a zig and now a zig-flower, as crimson reaches out along individual threads, web-like, before it blooms. A chevron-rose, and it is perfect.

Migraine

Warm fat drops hammer on my head, woodpecker knocking, no you cannot come in. Hot liquid metal glows behind my right optic window, hot and dry like the desert, lids scrap down and back up like window wipers on dry glass, screeeeech, shudders with resistance. Turn the monsoon off and step out into winter chill, bottom on ice-tiles, a shiver bubbles up my spine, slowly, vertebrae to vertebrae, then across my shoulders, skin prickles up, shiver extinguished by molten lava spilling from the pool traversing the tributaries on the right, perfect line separates east from west, territory charted, circumnavigated every few days. Gently, gently go to ground and press into the ceramic floor, resistance feels good, though stomach tide swells, surfs up, ride it out, as every breaking wave crashes first against the cliff top of my head, then kicks inside my gut. Vision turns indigo, fuzzy blurred lines surround me, and I groan, pulling the towel down around my body, cocooned for the longest time, I wait to emerge from my chrysalis.

Nervous world

Tiptoe, gently go. Jump at the siren, jump at the neighbour shouting, ranting. So much anger for one so young. So I tiptoe, gently go, past the window, to the bookshelf, so silent (until they open), fingertips across the spines, which one, which one, whisper to me, call and I will answer, hold you like a baby bird fallen from a tree, pick me, pick me and calm the sea of thoughts. Flashing lights burst around pulled blinds, boney fingers poke me in the eyes, neon nails of blue and red, conversation crescendo on the other side. No tiptoe, gently go, no not the neighbour, never will he ever, loud crash, door shouts shut. Baby bird in my hands, answer to my prayers. I open wide, walk right inside and tiptoe, gently go into another world where drama closes in but never reaches out for me, lives in front of me, cannot touch me. Fold the world in on itself, when reality is safe again, for me to tiptoe, gently go, nervous in this world.

Life on the edge

You and me on the horizon, we travel far from here, tiny dots disappearing into the line, ready to drop right off the edge. Edge, it's where we live, our edges, they're rough, jagged, sharp to the world but you and me on the horizon know just how to handle them, no blood drawn, no injury for us. This world is flat, flat earth for us, not that kind, we're not silly, we know our science, read all those books, but it's a flat earth from which we slip, if we, you and me on the horizon, don't watch our minds, we'll be in all kinds of binds, where there's no lines, not for you and me on the horizon, patiently waiting, take our meds, watching and waiting right on the edge. Don't fall over, try to stay, keep me company right here, sit down and I'll get you a beer. We'll share a smoke, a joke and be okay, keep on our travels, negotiating the tight-rope edge. It's just where we live, right here on the edge.

Check out my heart

You took my heart and stamped it 'due date', you borrowed it for a time. I consented, this is true, but I was so in love with you, there was nothing I would not do, as long as I could be with you. You returned it early, no late penalty to apply, you'd already checked out someone else's heart. I sat on the shelf, surprised when you returned to browse. Finding me you skimmed for a familiar passage but I wanted to show you something new, pages unseen, updated, expanded, now for modern times. I used my razor crisp new pages to slice your finger, to watch you bleed the way I had, and with a new, reinforced spine I snapped shut and bruised your knuckles and now you'll not come back looking for the past. I'm a big book now, I choose my own adventures.

Amble

I take the road others avoid. There's no destination. Success is another day. Don't look on me with pity, I never travel, I stay local. The village hermit. But I know the things you do not. You don't stop to marvel like I do. Stop to tie my shoe, to breath seaweed air hung with frangipani lace, touch the blade of grass so straight, so green, ever so vivid. Walk on, walk with me, I'll let you see the world from my eyes, hidden behind lens and coatings, protected, delicate. Step off with me, it's a mere five hundred metres, that's enough. Same route everyday. Days as different as new found paths. Never bored. Blue wren today, delicate-twitch in dust-laden beams shot through trees. A bleached-pacifier, aged yet new today. The ground constantly working our waste from deep hiding. Do you see the cars going by, their colours, their speed, patterns on plates? This path is an information overload - if you're open, receptive, a sponge. Fully engorged with sensory detail I turn and walk home but you carry on, haven't seen enough. You never opened your eyes.

Words and memory

Is there any point to words on the page? It's something I have to do, the only way I remember, and make sense of each day, each moment, each page is a window into the daily one inch picture frame I look through at the daisy in the rain, the sun that hides the pain, the cars hurtling past, the moon's light cast. It's how I find you in all of these things, your presence transcends day and night, the seasons that turn and the years that click over. When I look into her face, toddler, child, woman, mother, I see you, it's you looking back at me and I smile inside. Somewhere, out there, under a different light, do you see her, see me, like I see you on the page, words become your stage, since you became a memory.

Liquid lady

You're a heat seeking missile, darting up the passage, up on the tip-tops of cupboards, glaring down at me. Your eyes are moons, deep pools, and you don't suffer fools. Click and the blanket light's aglow. Can you smell heat? Ears erect and tail goes high, bent for speed you bounce down, beeline to warm your ass. Push me, tell me, in no uncertain terms, this blanket is yours and I'm just the one with opposable thumbs. Thank me with your purr, nip me, back off, personal space. You spread your self like liquid Burmese chocolate— melting, puddle ever larger.

Addiction

Screw your pills and powder, glinting liquids and phallic mouth-toys all. She's sleek, and shiny and she likes it when I dress her up. Crystals and gold, Egyptian cats, golden crowns. She's easily turned on, always ready for my touch, caresses sweet in the street and she doesn't care. Curled like a foetus against the world I'm not ready to face and she's contained within my space, she holds space big enough to fit the whole world, and I never turn my back on her in bed, I couldn't if I tried, though I've never felt inclined. Sometimes I lose touch with her as I sleep, but in half-light-wake my fingers stretch out and feel for her, close around and hold tight. She brightens to my touch, ever so slight, still she responds. She's an addition, an intimate addiction feeding my brain all the feel good hormones of warm liquid intoxication, of the needle in the vein, of that pill on my tongue, but without the compromise. Until next year, then my mind will wander, and my fingers long to touch another, to upgrade my love, renew my addiction. She's the apple of my eye.

The rapids

You and I sit with rushing rapids between our chairs. Danger, danger, caution! You and I so close and yet... what of this space between us. Television numbs the room, the balm of our lives, joined as one and yet... reaching out our fingers barely touch. War, weapons, women's rights, the presenter chants them all, and I open my mouth to speak, to salve the pain of the nightly news and yet... would I have to shout across this space, this void that sits between us? Feline fun, and playtime comes, she jumps from chair to chair, pet here, pet there, such silky hair she alone can cross those rushing rapids between these chairs and yet... we've had other pets, it's been years, and the space between was not always this wide and dangerous.

Writing

Dance, my fingers across the keys. Trance, my eyes see only the screen. This is what it feels like to be a writer. I don't understand the sipping of designer coffee watching people. Why would I need to describe so many ways to interact with coffee? Walk alone, breathe deep, stride short. That's the way I fill my well. I tried the meditation bell, it was what the book advised. Fidget, thoughts bounce around, stop! I need a pen. Too many thoughts, words describing each sensation, oily fingertips leave shining moons on keys, and blue-black ink burrows under fingernails. And yet I've starred out the window watching the wind muss the tree, without tapping a single key, the moss on the roof next door a vibrant yellow, and I now melancholy.

What Cupid did next

Tell me a secret and I'll tell you one too, confess to each other things that are true, so I told you I did it, and I had no regrets, but the one action beget a whole string, and it's the string I want shortened, to wipe from the past, and it's the string I won't tell you despite how you ask. It's worse than a virus, it's poison if shared and so I shake my head laughingly like I never did care. What one does for a lover, when love's at an end is always the worse kind of secret to have while you mend. It's Cupid's last laugh, he's wicked that way, not half as romantic as people will say. He'll have you bounce cheques, and be partners in crime, when partnership has fallen way down the line. So I'll tell you just part of my secret, and keep most of it hidden, lest it infect leaving this over before it begins.

Neighbour

Alone. He works alone. Watching the neighbour and her ant-line of visitors. He turns the ratchet slowly, stretching the winding sound long into the air. Resistance. Greasy fingers find the next piece of his puzzle without looking down. That one just now, he looks like trouble, bouncing on the balls of his feet, one hand exploring the texture of a stubble covered head while the other rolls a lighter to life over again. Their eyes meet, he looks down at the engine, it's really quite pretty, all Chevy orange, home painted V8, polished stainless steel that's never quite cold to his fingers. Someone calls out, wishes the woman happy seventieth grammy, and he sighs. Be darned if we don't share the day. He jostles metal through his fingers, pliers in hand, nips off some daisy, American beauty geranium too, lays them aside with a smile, and remembers his mother.

Fade away

Cream coloured paper, with the smell of fresh potted blue-black ink, the kind her father used to write with. It's one of the smells that transcend time. The other is silverside. Odd for a vegetarian. Still she knew her father cooked it best. The pen scratches out her thoughts, marks of this time, this day, when she wanted to be close to sun bleached memories, to secure them before fading to white. His face, what did his face look like? So difficult to recall. A water bead snakes down the page, ink scratch blooms like moss on wood. Frustration, what kind of a daughter can't recall what her father looked like? She could pass him on the street and not know. It hits her like a knife hits cheese, resistance, futile. You can't see the dead on the street.

Freedom

Escape with me, let's run until our spines uncurl and shoulders retreat from kissing chins day and night. Until we're no longer huddled over blue-light-warmth seeking solidarity in solitary confinement. Come with me and let's unfurl our limbs and clammer for dry land lest we sink in the mire we were forced into, a pool of tepid sludge we've insulated ourselves with, its alcohol-sterile smell feasts in nasal cavities. We can move beyond this time, this space, this time no longer recognised by me. I reach out, wind rushing against my face, eyes dry as desert sand, that's the rush that comes with living, when we do it right. That white knuckled sprint to freedom, will see us live again without digital dependancies, our only contact across the seas. But you and me, we'll escape, for at our core we are free, even if for now I hold you, aglow, in my hand, oblong tears, fingertips to screen, waiting on a vaccine, against Covid-19.

Travel

We stand together, they say, and we did believe, once, that it was true. Now, not so much, cancelled plans and conspiracy theories seemingly out of the blue. You tell me it's just a cold, but your aunty, yeah she was old, it killed her, you never got to travel to her, the boarders too tight, it's not right, this isn't how we knew life, new-life that we live now, in this expanse of island we're used to road trips, drop of a hat trips, now what was once hop, skip and jump, is beyond legal limits. How did we get here and yet can't get there anymore? Is it messing with your mind the way it is with mine? Maybe that's why you tell me stories that couldn't possibly be true, and I feel so blue, in my house where Plath's Bell Jar descends, hovers, shimmers, above my head until the morning, news and toast, and I didn't bother getting dressed again today… I wait, hoping to break five kms, might I start the car today? Drive a little way, just out the road, hop, skip and a jump - tiny travel is still travel.

White picket fences

Looking at an old photograph, fussy edged image, your smile so distinct, I forget why we fought, why I tore this photograph all those years ago when I thought life without you would fall into dust, it's been twenty five years since your smile was so near and I laugh as I think back, to times I felt myself shine, all aglow with young love and delusions of white picket fences and a trio of kids. I was sold on the dream of a home in the 'burbs and a mum-car. Instead I birthed knowledge and drive what I please, for here I am with all my degrees, two cats and a rented flat where I forget what it is I'm meant to regret.

Home 1/9

The one place I call my home, four walls and a warm heart, is living someone else's life. Two decades on, memories stuck like molluscs on pipe, barnacles on my brain, screaming come back, and I want to return to the past, the home, the one I left behind running from emotions and responsibility. Every house I've camped in since, four walls and a heart of stone, never yielding to me, no warmth to hold me lost at sea. I hadn't been looking for home, just running with new found freedom, coming of age in a hurricane of new possibilities, and then the baby came, she cemented the four walls as what I would always know as home, much more conceived inside to set that warm home-heart beating.

(Re)housing

    Bricks the colour of my coffee, tiled green roof and so much beige, beige as far as the eye can see. You see a tired decor, you see why the rent isn't as high as it might have been. I see the inside of my heart, rooms like chambers beat, holding my life inside, delicate and strong, memories made and yet to be made pump through the circuitry, ready for me to plug back in, an appliance, replaceable if I should malfunction, and I did, all those years ago. I've been away for repairs for twenty years and now refurbished, I return, eager to pick up where I left off. I say I can forget the others if you can too, these rooms will hold more than my heart, my insecurities. This time I promise to be faithful.

Sweaty sheets

Little bow lips, wet-yellow, sweet-sour breath escapes, you shudder and relax in my arms. At once I am so fully in love that I finally understand all the angsty songs of my teens but I also recognise the potential this relationship has for abuse and wonder if one of us will need to learn to duck and weave, to deflect pointy words and razor sharp names as time elapses and we grow comfortable in this new dynamic. I've never been in this kind of relationship before, it scare-thrills me. I am no longer me, singular, defined on my own terms, but I am a half of our we and I'm not sure if I want to be defined by my relationship to you. Is it a bad sign for us that even as I lay beside you I already resent you, your presence, your hold over me, just a little? Without you I could be in a city far from here, in a nightclub, a drink dancing in my head, and me on tabletop, but because of you there's no last minute trip across this wide country to find hedonist decadence at the bottom of a glass, no drink me, eat me, and down the rabbit hole. I am here because of you, your hold, and I worry. How did a hand the size of my little finger, grip my heart and mind so tight that I'm happy with this silence, the rise and fall of your chest and sour milk soaked sheets in this heat?

Teach me

I see the boy with the strawberry blonde hair, and he raises a dimpled hand in the air, leans in, just a bit, and his expression warps from childhood innocence to all teeth and menacing, feet slow stomping on honey wood flooring, echoing dinosaur roars, then stops, straightens, childlike once more, 'Nan, 'saurs?' And I'm young again, under the dining table, stalked by T-rex, folded in on myself, Shhhh, hiding! Laughter and love come from so far down it's in my toes, radiates to my eyes, and I can't stop, won't stop smiling. I'd forgotten how to play, how to frolic, how to be carefree. My teacher is two and so far ahead of me, but has no degree. This student has much to learn, to learn to be free.

Reflections

In his little face I see the past, my past and it can no longer be denied. It's never spoken of, youthful mistakes are to be forgiven and soon forgotten, but mine stares back at me, smiles and giggles and reminds me of you. I saw you there and wondered if you'd possessed this little child to visit a time or two with me. It's silly I know to think of you that way. We live in times so deliberate that chance DNA reflections seem unlikely. Look back, I try to look back, and when I do I fall down that rabbit hole of past meets present and love meets loss and you and I and what came from a short time of love. Yes, she came from a love, a young and foolish love. Now history repeats and here's a fresh face radiating your smile back at me and asking 'whatswrong?' And tapping my head with dimpled hands neither yours nor mine nor her just his.

Let her speak

She curls into herself, phone a glow, memories like fiery darts landing across the rocky terrain of her battle weary mind, and she remembers his smile, that smirk, such a jerk, the way he said there's no evidence, no proof of his offence, and yet it replays in high definition, with instant recognition, over and over while she waits for the time to pass until she picks up her kid, their kid, again, and has to stand there, toe to toe, face to face, and she smiles, always, for their kid, she smiles, like it has long been washed off and send down the shower drain, and that smile is such a strain, face to face with the perpetrator, the common denominator in their separation, always it is him. Right now she wonders who to reach out to, to text, call, Skype, message, snap, so many choices but they're tired of hearing her complain, the same refrain but I don't want my kid to have a dad in jail… shouldn't she be over it? Why does she still wake up as if it's happening again, wet face, silent scream, just like then, don't wake the baby, the tiny baby, no longer a baby, but she hasn't moved on and there's no one left to text, call, Skype, message, snap, and she just might snap, she feels one day, in the waiting she may curl so far into herself, around this comforting glow, that her body might just snap in on itself and join her mind. Would he be remorseful then?

Messages

Pull your skirt down, don't show your knickers, don't sit on his knee, sit with your legs together, that skirt is too short, don't send the wrong idea, the wrong signal, don't lead him on, don't provoke him, don't be provocative, promiscuous, you'll get a reputation, don't go out without a bra, don't tell suggestive jokes, or use explicit language, it's a daisy, a flower, a front bottom, it's a private, a virtue, something to be lost on your wedding night. I was born with space between my legs. The mark of an assault waiting to happen, impending, never ending messages of what is proper, how to prevent being attacked. Can't I just say two letters, together, no, just the once, and it be respected, I be respected, my body be respected? It's a small message, a message that lets childhood be carefree where I hang upside down on monkey bars, turn dizzy cartwheels with pride and grace, remove the self-conscious fear of the impending puberty my tiny breasts foreshadow. A message that takes less energy than the constant barrage of stay-safe rules that tells us we're in faux-control, the one that tells us it's our fault when it happens, and it happens far too much. The simple message, no, is the one I want, the one that should give me control. I should have control, be in control, of me, of my body, this body with the space, that should not signal an attack. No.

Cat life

I measure my life by the nine lives of each cat who keeps me company. The tuxedoed boy, with his monkey tail signals times of liberty and laughter, love and seduction, of one hot mess body slamming another, of reproductive rights exercised, marked off on calendars, timed, specific, mechanical. He marks the house that's home, the ones before and after, he measures independence. The white and tabby that came next showed what second chances were all about, and rigid schedules to sleep and eat, of worship times, exchanged vows, and what a fragile eggshell mental health can be, when it's not yours, just conjoined, that vow to keep. The brown Burmese measured teenage angst and hard rebellion that bought fiery arrows raining down, of empty nest and more housing without stability, she measures the grey streaks, we're going grey together, she doesn't like it if you point it out and she hides from the new baby, grand baby, hisses when he cries. Will the next cat in line, with nine lives spent see mine spent with it?

Stop the rock

Pulling on the evening stockings, sheer over stubble, a porcupine wrapped up, seams made straight and Mary Jane's on feet. Cli-op, cli-op, floorboards slip-shined that very day in bare legs and naked feet. Daily work complete, reward, out the door, down to the street and cli-ek, cli-ek, city of white-noise swims around me, surrounds me. Breathe, as I weave between mister brief-case-going-home, and missus I'm-on-the-phone, eyes forward, duck and weave while they don't see, me cli-at, cli-at, dodge him, dodge her, dodge a cat, sashaying east, past my feet. Smooth the satin over tulle, posture firm and I am off to learn with a cle-it, cle-it, once a week, to the hall where we meet. Cli-up, cli-up, I'll end up in stocking feet, after the first twirl, still I'll beam, with crocked seams, when we rock we don't stop, won't stop, can't stop. Rock around the clock.

Teen angst

Shimmering vampires and blood red hair, no parenting book had me prepared. What was a MySpace and how did I find one, party like a rockstar and what did that say? I'm open and liberal and don't want to set rules, but I feel suddenly old and without the right tools. Nocturnal texting and school notes about sexting. Why am I shocked, I had *The Story of my Life,* hidden from sight, right next to my cigarettes and Harley Davidson lighter, and while I wasn't a fighter, they just seemed to find me. I pieced my ears with a sewing room needle, always drinking by six and sober by curfew. Thank God for no internet and cameras were few, so I can deny any crime, how about you?

Merry music maid

The melody breaks through my thoughts of bread, chocolate and toilet paper. It rattles in my ears, up into my brain, down to the depths of memory, of memoria, where you dwell now, since October 18, the day you stopped being that person I needed to remember to message, to call, mobile love, distance no deficit, and now you're filed away until the merry music maid drops into the files and pulls you out to dance decadently deep inside me. You were always pretty enough, and you were bitch, mother, daughter, lover and you were like no other, and nothing compared to you. My friend, my sister from another mister, as you'd say. Any of these songs make me stop, and let that merry music maid wait on me until the corners on my lips dip up and down unsure, is this where I laugh or where I cry, right here in the store with such important things to do. I think I'll choose to smile this time.

www.ingramcontent.com/pod-product-compliance
Lightning Source LLC
Chambersburg PA
CBHW022023290426
44109CB00015B/1285